*Where Do I Go
from Here?*

Where Do I Go from Here?

*Now That You've Given your Heart
and Life to Jesus, What's Next?*

Lucrecia Garcia

WestBow
PRESS
A DIVISION OF THOMAS NELSON

NLT—New Living Translation
Scripture quotations taken from the Holy Bible, New Living
Translation, copyright 1996, 2004. Used by permission of Tyndale
House Publishers, Inc., Wheaton, Illinois 60189. All rights reserved.

WestBow Press books may be ordered through
booksellers or by contacting:

WestBow Press
A Division of Thomas Nelson
1663 Liberty Drive
Bloomington, IN 47403
www.westbowpress.com
1-(866) 928-1240

ISBN: 978-1-4908-0348-7 (sc)
ISBN: 978-1-4908-0349-4 (e)

Library of Congress Control Number: 2013913609

Printed in the United States of America.

WestBow Press rev. date: 7/31/2013

Dedication

I dedicate this book first to my Lord and Savior, Jesus, and then to my family—my amazing husband and wonderful children. To David, my first baby, whose God-given musical talents and dedication to the Lord, have blessed many. To my baby girl, Lisa, thank you for your strong commitment to the Lord and for all the comfort and encouragement you've given me through the years. To Michael, my last baby, thank you for all the joy and laughter you have brought to Dad and me when we needed them. And to all my beautiful grandchildren who give me so much unconditional love!

Contents

Welcome to the Family of God

Congratulations! You have just made the most important decision of your life! You got saved. Saved from what? Saved from a life of hopelessness, defeat, depression, sickness, and eternal separation from God. Now you need to know more about this great God who loves you and gave His life to forgive you, bless you and have a relationship with you.

"So where do I go from here?" you are probably asking yourself. Well, maybe I can help you. In this booklet, we will cover some basic, simple steps to starting and living an exciting, victorious Christian life. Yes, God coming into your life is the most exciting thing that can happen to anyone! I have been a Christian for many years and have learned a lot. Some things I learned the hard way. But no matter how long you live for God, there's always more and more to learn, which makes the Christian life exciting. However, in this book I have attempted to provide you with some shortcuts that took me many years to learn. I've tried to put your new life in a nutshell, so to speak, to give you a running start to the most exciting journey you will ever encounter.

Let's start at the beginning, when God created the earth as we know it. As you may know God is a three-part being—God the Father, God the Son, and God the Holy Spirit—but He is one God, also known as the Trinity. Look at it this way: you can take one apple and cut it into three pieces. It would still be one apple, though, just in three pieces. Well, that's similar to what God says He is. Right now God the Father is in heaven, Jesus is seated at His right hand, and the Holy Spirit is here on earth with us and in us. The Holy Spirit is just as much God as Jesus and the Father. Cool.

In the beginning, the Lord created the garden of Eden with everything in it humanity would ever need. It was perfect. Then He created Adam and Eve to live in the garden of Eden so He could share His creation with people. The book of Genesis tells us the Lord Himself would walk in the garden and fellowship with Adam and Eve. However, one day the Devil, in the form of the serpent, caused Adam and Eve to sin against God when they ate the forbidden fruit. Because of their disobedience, the Lord removed them from the garden. Therefore, they passed a sinful nature—a desire to sin—down to us.

We are born with that sin nature. That's why my nine-month-old granddaughter beat on her twin nine-month-old brother when he took her toy. Nine months old and she knew how to inflict pain to get what she wanted! Where did she get that from? It's that sinful nature, kiddo.

Sin leads to death—eternal separation from God. God is holy, and He cannot tolerate sin. Therefore, because of the actions of one man, Adam, all of humankind was separated from God, but the good news is that through one man, Jesus Christ, humankind was reunited with God. Jesus came to remove that separation and bring us back to God. What the Lord wanted then, and still wants with us today, was an intimate relationship with His creation. He can't have that with animals. They were not created in His image. Only we were created to be like Him and act like Him. You and I are His children.

So God came up with a plan. It all started with Jesus dying on the cross so you and I could be forgiven of *all* of our sins and could have a relationship with the living God. Only the blood of Jesus can remove—not cover, remove—our sins. The Bible says, "For *everyone* has sinned. We all fall short of God's glorious standard" (Romans 3:23 NLT). So you see, you've got a lot of company.

However, God also said, "And *God* has piled all our sins, everything we've done wrong, *on Him* (Jesus)" (Isaiah 53:6 MSG). Before Jesus came, thousands of years ago, if you disobeyed God, you had to kill a perfect lamb or a perfect goat as a sacrifice to God to pay for your sin. If that was still true today, imagine the mess we'd have in our backyards! There had to be bloodshed. God didn't punish the offender; He punished the animal. Jesus, His Son, was the ultimate sacrifice. Now there is no more sacrifice of animals.

But God the Father wanted more than that. He wanted that personal, intimate relationship with His children. For that to happen, He had to live inside of us because we needed help, so He sent part of Himself—His Holy Spirit—to live inside of us. That's why when you sincerely give your life to Jesus, you feel so different. It's the precious Holy Spirit inside of you.

Now I've got to share a Scripture that probably is the first Scripture every Christian memorizes. It says, "For God loved the world so much that he gave his one and only Son, so that everyone who believes in him will not perish but have eternal life" (John 3:16 NLT). That's how much God loves you and me.

Jesus shed His blood—once and for all. He was sinless and the perfect Lamb of God who came to take our place—our punishment—on the cross so all we need to do is go to our Father in the name of Jesus to be forgiven when we sin. So look at it this way—God punished Himself for your and my mess.

Wow! What a loving God! That's why John 3:3 says we must be born again. Being born again means just that. Our inner person (our spirit) is reborn, and that is the part of us that changes. The Bible says we are a spirit, we live in a body, and we have a mind (soul). Our body and mind remain the same. If you were tall or skinny, you will still be tall or skinny after you get saved. If you were good-looking, you are still good-looking. As for your mind, it remains the same too. You can remember your name and everything else that was in your brain.

However, God says to read His book and you will learn to think like Him by renewing your mind. When our spirits leave our bodies, what happens to our bodies? They die. But our spirits (the real you) return to God (or head in the other direction) because our spirits are eternal. They live forever, either in heaven or in hell.

I was terrified of death when I didn't know the Lord. I was young, but man I was so afraid to die! I didn't know for sure, but I believed that dying was not the end of it and my spirit was going to go somewhere I wasn't going to like. I didn't know what to do about it. But on the night I got saved—gave my life to Jesus—all that fear disappeared. I no longer fear death. Don't misunderstand me—I don't have a death wish. I have a lot I still want to accomplish for God before I go. But I know that I know that I know that when I leave this earth, I will be with my Lord forever, and so will you! Nobody had to tell me this. I just knew it.

What this means is that you and I have a new life! All of the old things have passed away. Everything has become new. He created us in His image—to look and act like Him. You are His child, and He loves you so. Truly *our God is an awesome God!*

And you know what's also so great? Once you ask God to forgive you, He removes your sins as far as the east is from the west and remembers them no more. God says He will *no longer* remember your mistakes or your past. Do you know that God the Father loves you as much as He loves Jesus? That's right! It's in His book. Giving your life to Christ means you are now an heir to the blessings of God, and He will take care of you for the rest of your life. And no one can care for you the way He does! I know that from personal experience.

Let me tell you what happened to me. Many years ago, I had an abortion because my life was an absolute mess, and I didn't know which way to turn. The church I was married in (but didn't really attend) taught that if you had an abortion, you were on a roller coaster to *hell*! There was *no* forgiveness for you, so you shouldn't even bother to come back to church. Nice, huh?

I felt so guilty and started to hear voices telling me I was worse than a murderer because murderers murder sinners. I had murdered an innocent baby. Every night I would have horrible nightmares about what I had done. In some of the nightmares, I was bathed in blood. The Devil was torturing me. It was like I was carrying a big, heavy cross. I didn't know Jesus had carried it for me!

I lived with this guilt for several months, and honestly, I contemplated suicide many times because I believed what I was told—that there was no hope for me, that God didn't love me or want me. The only reason I didn't kill myself was because I had a beautiful three-year-old son who I knew needed his mommy. Guess that's why that boy is still special to me. What a crock of lies! If you are reading this and someone told you that junk, well, hallelujah, help has arrived, and His name is Jesus! There's forgiveness in Jesus *no matter what you have done!*

It's a long story I'll tell you some other time, but one night I visited a "real" church, and for the first time in my life, I heard the pastor say that *no matter what you have done, God will forgive you.* I couldn't believe what I was hearing. *Could that be true?* I asked myself.

"Do you want to be forgiven?" the pastor said. "Come to this altar, and someone will pray with you."

As he continued to talk, I felt drawn to the church altar, like a magnet was pulling me, so I yielded to that drawing and went to the altar, where someone did pray for me to receive Jesus as my Savior. They never asked me what I had done wrong, and you know what? As long as God knows, that's all that matters. As I was praying with this person, I actually felt the weight that was on my shoulders disappear! That was my first miracle! *Wow,* I thought. *God, you must be very powerful.* And He is. That night I left that church a brand new person. For the first time, I heard birds singing, and my life took a radical change for the best (not better). Praise the Lord!

So how do you start your new life? This new life is a journey, and the end of the journey is when we get to heaven. But meanwhile, what a wonderful journey it is! I'm not trying to tell you that you will not face challenges and mountains. We are not in heaven yet where everything is perfect. Oh yeah, some things are going to go wrong. The Devil will make sure of that. But read on. It's good; it's all good. As you begin this new journey, let's look at some simple steps.

Step 1

Start to Read Your Bible

The Bible (the Word) was written by men under the inspiration (leading) of the Holy Spirit as a book written to you and me. In it the Lord reveals Himself and His great love for us. He tells us how to live a life that overcomes all the challenges we face. Yes, you will face problems just like anyone else. But you have a God, *unlike anyone else who is not a Christian*, who will help you, guide you, heal you, deliver you, and bless you if you listen to Him and do it His way.

Maybe like me you too were living a life of despair, hurt, and pain, but Jesus said, "Come to me, all of you who are weary and carry heavy burdens, and I will give you rest" (Matthew 11:28 NLT). In the Bible, He gives us words of guidance and instructions as to how to live with Him the best life we could possibly have. Jesus said, "In this godless world you will continue to experience difficulties. But take heart! I've conquered the world" (John 16:33 MSG). He conquered the world for us so that when we pray in His name, we will come out of our situations as winners. When you read the last book of the Bible, the book of Revelation, you see that we win! We may struggle, but when we persevere and believe God, we always win! You see, this world still belongs to the Devil. The Bible calls him the "god of this world." But Jesus has delivered us from *all* of the Devil's power. **"For He (Jesus) has rescued us from the kingdom of darkness and transferred us into the Kingdom of his dear Son, who purchased our freedom and forgave our sins"** (Colossians 1:13-14 NLT).

He will try to hurt us, depress us, and make us sick, but Jesus has delivered us (those who have received Jesus as Lord and Savior and are living for Him) from the powers of darkness. Oh yes, the Devil still has power but not over believers!

The gospel of John is a great place to begin reading your Bible. That's the third book in the New Testament, and it's all about Jesus! The book of John is an easy-to-read account of the life of Jesus. Let me explain. Even though the Bible is one book, it contains sixty-six small books written by forty authors over a span of nearly sixteen hundred years. However, every book agrees with the others, and it contains no errors or contradictions. Pretty amazing, huh! Historically, the Bible continues to be the best-selling book of *all time*! According to an article from David Brandt Berg and the Family International, Deep Truths, www.deeptruths.com, "The Bible has been read by more people than any other book. It has outsold every book that has ever been written and it *still* sells more copies every year than any other book in the World!"

Each book of the Bible has chapters and verses. Each chapter has a number, and so does each verse (so we can easily find them). For example, Genesis is the first book of the Bible, so Genesis 1:1 (NKJV) says, "In the beginning, God created the heavens and the earth" That's the first chapter and the first verse. Get it? Don't worry! You'll get the hang of it.

The Old Testament is *before* Jesus came to the earth, and the New Testament is *when* and *after* He came to the earth. It's all about Him. By the way, get yourself a Bible that is easy to understand. There are many great translations out there. Read through several of them at the Christian bookstore till you find one you are comfortable with. Then read at least one chapter *every day* and begin to learn who God is and His plan for you.

Reading the Word feeds us spiritually and makes us strong. We feed our bodies with food, but we also need to feed our spirits, and the Bible is that food. When you read your chapter, don't just rush through it, but think about it, meditate on it, and let it take root in your heart, believing it. "For as he thinks in his heart, so is he" (Proverbs 23:7 NKJV). When you read a Scripture that blesses you, write it down and put it on your refrigerator, on your desk, or on your bathroom mirror. Then keep reading it and standing on God's promise to you.

The Word is a seed that you plant in your heart, and it will grow and change the way things work in your life. The written Word of God is one of the most powerful weapons we can use against the Devil when he tries to bring us problems (sickness, depression, lack, strife). You can remind him of what you read in the Bible—that you have authority over him and it's God's will to bless you. Speak God's Word out loud to your circumstances and Jesus said those mountains will move! He promises that if we have faith, the mountains have no choice but to move! God is on your side!

I was a Christian for many years and had read the Bible from cover to cover a few times, but I never really devoted myself to studying it. I just knew enough of the Bible to get by. I knew about faith and believing God for miracles, and I saw miracles in my life. But I was missing walking in victory in many other areas because I didn't really know the promises that were mine! Many Christians are like I used to be and don't know the blessings God has for them because they don't read their Bibles. Don't be one of them!

No one told me what I am telling you. I not only read but also study the Bible every day because I am retired and have lots of time. However, no matter how busy you are, come on—you can spare fifteen minutes a day to pray and read one chapter! *Do it!* The Devil knows that when you know what belongs to you, you will put *chichones* on his ugly head (that's Spanish for knots). He tries to keep you from reading the Bible. He will create all kinds of distractions. Don't let him! Make time for God and your rewards will be great!

You can go online (google it) and get a Bible-reading plan where you can read your Bible in six months, a year, two years— whatever! You can also read your Bible online on your smartphone or iPad. All of the promises God has made *to you* are in

His book—to love you, to bless you, to heal you, to prosper you, and to protect you. But how can you claim them if you don't know what they are?

Step 2

Pray

Okay, now that He is living in you, you need to talk to Him. Prayer is just talking to God. No fancy words. No fancy sayings. You don't have to have the exact perfect words (they don't exist). It's just you and your heavenly Father having a conversation. To have a relationship with God, or anyone, for that matter, you need to talk to them. If you never talked to your spouse or your friends, you wouldn't have much of a relationship. Well, the Lord wants so much to hear from you! Pick a place where there are no distractions. Set aside just fifteen minutes a day to talk to God and read one chapter of the Bible.

God says in Psalm 1:1 that blessed is the man (or woman) who meditates (thinks about) the Scriptures day and night. I promise you, it will change your life. This is how you start. In the morning before you start your day, in the evening before bed, maybe during lunchtime at work, or any other time you can be alone with Him, pick up your Bible and do as follows.

Thank Him for All He Has Done

Spend the first few minutes thanking Him! Psalm 100:4 tells us to go before Him with thanksgiving and praise. Here's an example: "Father, I come to you in the name of Jesus." Jesus said to use His name when we pray to the Father. "Thank you for saving me, loving me, changing my life, and all you have given me, such as _____, etc."

Tell Him All You Need

Then for the next few minutes, tell Him what you need. Open your heart and talk to Him as you would talk to your earthly father. Maybe, like me, you didn't have an earthly father. Well, God is your Father, and

He loves you and longs to hear you speak to Him.

Although He already knows what you need, He wants to hear from you. Look at this cool promise Jesus said in Matthew 7:7-8 (NKJV): *"Ask* and it *will* be given to you. *Seek* and you *will* find. *Knock* and the door *will* be opened to you. For *everyone* who asks *receives*, and he who *seeks*, *finds*, and to him who *knocks*, it will be *opened."* Hallelujah! That's God's promise that when we pray and believe He has heard us, He answers.

He will speak to you in your spirit. As you grow in the Lord, you will become more and more sensitive to His voice. He said His sheep (you and I) hear His voice, and we know Him. That small, still voice inside of you is the Holy Spirit guiding you. Remember this—that voice will always agree with the Bible. God will never tell you anything crazy that does not agree with His written Word. Any voice you hear inside of you that does not agree with the Bible is not God, and you must reject it. That's why you need to read your Bible and attend a church where you can learn all of these things.

Praise Him for Hearing You and Answering Your Prayers

Thank Him because by faith you know He has heard you.

Enjoy Him by Reading One Chapter

Like I explained earlier, start with the book of John or anywhere else you feel comfortable. The book of Psalms in the Old Testament is also a cool book. The important thing is just to read! Don't forget about Him. All day long, think about Him. Take a few seconds during the day to tell Him you love Him, and ask Him to help you with the tasks and challenges you might be facing that day. He says in Proverbs 3:6 to include Him in your daily doings, and He promises to direct you and guide you!

These four guidelines should take you about fifteen to twenty minutes and will result in many benefits and blessings! Our Father in heaven honors our sacrifices when we put Him first.

Find a Good Church

Going to church helps you several ways:

- You get stronger in your faith as you hear the Word of God being spoken.
- You meet fellow believers.
- You can attend Bible studies and learn more about the authority and power God has given you.

When you look for a church, make sure it is a Bible-believing church where God the Father, God the Son, and God the Holy Spirit are worshipped. There are no perfect churches, of course, because there are no perfect people. But there must be preaching from the Bible, and everything you hear *must* agree with the Bible. Take your Bible to church and read for yourself the Scriptures you hear. You also should see people get saved and people get healed and delivered in almost every service. The pastor should regularly open the altar for anyone who would like to be prayed for. Hey, sometimes we all need someone else to pray for us, and that's okay.

Also, the church should be involved in supporting other ministries either locally or in other parts of the world. The church that does this is blessed. The church I attend recently received five tractor trailer truckloads of donated food from a food chain. They distributed the items to many others and kept some in their warehouse to continue to feed the people in the church and community. Every church should be reaching out to the community in some way.

Also, the church should have good worship music so you as the worshipper can feel the presence of God. That's very important. Let me explain the difference between praise and worship. One of the definitions of the word *praise* is to thank. When you praise the Lord, you are singing lively, fast songs and thanking Him for *what*

He has done and will do for you. That's why most music services in church start out with fast songs and then move to slower songs.

Worship means to adore. When you worship the Lord, you are singing slower songs, and you enter into a time of intimacy where you are loving Him for *who He is*. Oh yeah. Miracles take place when the church begins to sing and worship the Lord because God inhabits (stays) in the praises of His people. His presence is *always* with you because He lives inside of you, so you don't have to ask Him to come to you or touch you. The Holy Spirit is in you. He's always with you and touching you. But when we sing to our God, we can feel His presence move upon us and around us. It's awesome!

Ask the Lord to lead you to a church where you can find all of these things and be taught to live the victorious Christian life God wants you to have. Let Him guide you. The Holy Spirit who is now inside of you will speak to you. He wants you in a good church. You also will meet great Christian friends who will adopt you as their brother/sister in the Lord and love you. You become a part of God's family and can grow spiritually and learn more about God and all the good things He has for you. Also, you can go to your pastor or Bible teacher with questions about your newly found faith.

When you find a good church and should you need transportation, speak to the pastor or one of the leaders. Many churches have folks who carpool or have a church bus.

How often should you go to church? Good question. Let me give you my opinion. The Bible does *not* tell us how many times to attend church but it does say this: "And let us not neglect our meeting together, as some people do" (Heb. 10:25 NLT). To me, Sunday is the most important day because that's when we start the week off with God. We put Him first. Usually, your church will have a nice service planned with music and Bible preaching and prayer.

The mid-week service (some churches do Wednesdays, others do other nights) is next in importance. That's when there's usually a Bible study, and it's very important to attend that so you can learn a lot about the Word and ask questions, which helps you to mature spiritually. If your church has other services, they are usually optional.

The Lord does not keep a record of your church attendance, or He would tell us that in His Word. However, He expects us to attend church and to support our church. It pleases Him when we spend time in His presence, and attending church services is just that. So find a church that is on fire for God, is teaching the Bible and has exciting activities going on and above all, makes you feel good! Remember, ask the Lord to help you with this decision.

Step 4

Get Baptized in Water

You were saved when you confessed Jesus as your Savior. However, Jesus' disciples baptized believers and Jesus Himself set the example by being baptized. John the Baptist immersed in water those who came for baptism (head to toe), and that is how he baptized Jesus. That's how we need to be baptized. When Jesus allowed John the Baptist to baptize Him, He identified with the people He came to save. Jesus was sinless and didn't need to be baptized, but by doing so, He gave approval to John's ministry.

Being baptized in water is symbolic of your old life being buried in the water and you are coming up out of the water with a new life. Hallelujah! It shows your complete surrender to God. It's your public declaration that you love God and now you belong to Him!

So what happens if you don't get baptized in water? When Jesus was on the cross, there were two thieves, one on either side of Him. One of them asked Jesus to take him with Him. Jesus answered, "Today, you will be with me in Paradise" (Luke 23:43 NKJV). In other words, "Don't worry, my man. I've got ya." This man didn't get baptized in water, read his Bible, or do any of the other things God expects us to do. Well, duh, it's obvious he didn't have time to do any of that. He went to heaven without being baptized in water. Not being water baptized is not going to keep you out of heaven either. However, we have time, and for the duration of the years God has for us on this earth, Jesus asked us to do it, so we need to obey Him. We need to walk with Him closely so we can have that abundant life He promised to those who followed Him.

Ask your pastor when the next baptismal service will take place, and get baptized in water! You'll love it!

Step 5

Give God a Small Portion of Your Money

"Oh, no! Why do I have to give money?" You don't have to, but if you want even more blessings, you must obey the Lord. When you give God ten percent (a tithe) of your gross income (that's your earnings before any deductions are taken out), you enter into a contract (Malachi 3:10) with Him where He promises to give it back to you, several times over. You know He wants you to be prosperous because it makes our heavenly Father look good to have blessed children, and in turn you can bless those who are in need.

If you are a parent, you feel good when your children excel and look good. That's how our heavenly Father feels. The Lord says, "Let the Lord be magnified, Who has pleasure in the prosperity of His servant" (Ps.

35:27 NKJV). God loves to see us blessed. Also, the church uses the money you give to reach others who don't know Jesus and to meet the needs of the church. God will financially bless you! Not only does the Bible say this, but I am also speaking from experience.

Through my years walking with God, I have been faithful in giving my tithes to my local church and to other ministries. I have been greatly blessed. Years ago, my family and I went through a very difficult time due to our not listening to God. We financially lost everything. Although we had failed to listen to God, He rescued us! He forgave us and set us on the right path again. Today I can say that the Lord has given us more than *twice* what we lost. He never abandoned us, and we can truly say we are not only more blessed but happier than ever!

Well, there you have it—some basic steps for a victorious life. Living the Christian life is the most amazing thing you can do. Without Him, we just exist. When we give our lives to Him, He breathes life into our being, and we become alive.

Next, I am going to try to answer some questions you may have as a new believer. Here goes.

Frequently Asked Questions

Do I have to change anything or give up anything now that I'm saved?

Yes and no. The night my husband was going to be baptized in water at our church, he was still a smoker. He went to the pastor before the baptismal and asked him if he could still be baptized since he smoked. The very wise pastor said, "Son, don't worry about it. God will take the cigarettes away in time. Just trust Him."

And that's exactly how it happened. A short time later, he lost his desire for those cancer sticks and never smoked again. Sometimes it's hard to leave or break bad habits even though you know they are killing you. As a new believer, now the Holy Spirit is in you, and He is so very, very powerful and yet gentle. He will remove those desires and give you the strength to conquer them if you ask Him to and you mean business. He does the work. You just have to believe and trust Him.

What is faith?

The Bible says, "Faith is the confidence that what we hope for will actually happen. It gives us assurance about things we cannot see" (Hebrews 11:1 NLT). Even more simply put, faith is knowing that all of God's promises are true and are yours. So what can I say about faith? Every child of God has been given a measure (portion) of faith. The Bible says, "And it is impossible to please God without faith. Anyone who wants to come to Him must believe that God exists and that he rewards those who sincerely seek Him" (Hebrews 11:6 NLT). In everything we get from God, we have to use faith. You probably don't know this yet, but when you gave your life to Jesus, you used faith. Someone shared the good news with you that Jesus had died for you and therefore your sins were forgiven and you believed. Even though you did not see Jesus die on the Cross, you believed! You used your faith.

There are so many examples of faith in the Bible. Look at Hebrews 11:32-34 (NLT):

How much more do I need to say? It would take too long to recount the stories of the faith of Gideon, Barak, Samson, Jephthah, David, Samuel, and all the prophets. By faith these people overthrew kingdoms, ruled with justice, and received what God had promised them. They shut the mouths of lions, quenched the flames of fire, and escaped death by the edge of the sword. Their weakness was turned to strength. They became strong in battle and put whole armies to flight.

These are just some of the things faith in the Word of God accomplishes, and that means you! Yes, you can use your faith to receive all the things God has promised you.

As I told you, my family went through severe financial hardship. We had to file bankruptcy and were living in different rented houses for about seven years. We had lost jobs, the house we owned, cars, and money, but never our God. Eventually my husband and I both found full-time jobs, but finances were very tight. I longed to have my own home again, so I prayed and asked God for a house.

I knew He heard me because it is His will to bless us, so I never asked Him again but just thanked Him every day for my new home. "Ask and you shall receive," the Bible says, "for *everyone* who asks receives." Well, we found a lovely home in a great neighborhood, at a great price, but because of our poor credit, we did not qualify to look at any available homes, so we could not go inside the house. We could only look on the outside. We had absolutely no money and no credit to buy a house. But, I had faith, and that's all you need!

God had given me a tremendous peace that this was His will because it agreed with His Word that says He wants to bless us. We went to the bank and told them our situation—no money, no credit, but we had found a house. The banker was polite but offered us no help. I know he thought we were nuts, but I know a God who is mightier than any bank! We went back to the new house the next day and sat in the driveway for a few minutes just thanking the Lord for the house.

Let me explain something here. If the Lord would have had a better house for us, He would have told me. I wouldn't have felt such a peace about this house. But the peace I felt assured me I was in His will.

All of a sudden, the next-door neighbor came outside. He came over to us and asked if we were interested in the house. It had been vacant for several months, he said, and he knew the owner. He gave us the owner's phone number. Remember, we still had zero money and zero credit. We went home and called the owner.

The owner said, and I kid you not, "The house has been vacant for several months, and I am anxious to get rid of it. I own the home, my in-laws lived in it, and they now live near me, so make me an offer."

We said, "We don't have an offer," and explained our situation.

He said, "No problem. I own a small mortgage company, and I will finance the house for you. I am anxious to get rid of it. I just want you to buy it! Just bring your documents and come and see me."

Well, to make a long story short (I have a lot of long stories), we purchased that house with *no money* at the settlement table and horrible credit. Hallelujah! Praise the Lord! Within a few weeks, we were moving into our beautiful home. Oh, by the way, remember I didn't get to see the inside till shortly before the move, but I wasn't worried. God never gives junk! The inside was beautiful, just like I believed. All it needed was a cleaning and a few minor repairs. Wow, what a blessing! Five years later, we had established credit and sold the house at a nice profit and bought another house. Praise the Lord!

So you see, my friend, faith is the key that will unlock any door. But make sure what you are believing for is God's will and is in agreement with His Word. Please don't think you can use faith to rob a bank or do anything else that is illegal or immoral. You will not get that prayer answered! God promises us blessings, health, peace, victory in testings and trials, love, joy, protection, and many other things. He's not given us just faith but other weapons too that we can use to defeat the enemy every single time. More about that in another book.

What is communion?

The night before Jesus was crucified, He had the Last Supper with His disciples. As you probably know, this is where He shared the bread and the wine. Was it actual wine? Some say it was; others say it was unfermented wine, like grape juice.

Whether it was or was not is not important. It represents that precious blood Jesus shed for us so we could be free. Because many Christians who are ex-alcoholics partake of the communion and others prefer not to drink real wine, most churches have wisely chosen to use grape juice. Remember, it's symbolic of the sacrifice Jesus made for us. He told them to do this as a remembrance of Him. He said the bread loaf was to be broken and then shared among them because it represented His body, which was going to be broken for us. The wine represented the blood He was going to shed.

Some churches have communion once a month and others more often. It doesn't matter as long as we do it. You can do it on your own some time. But first examine your heart for anything that you may have done wrong and ask the Lord to forgive you, before you take any communion. Then, do like Jesus did. Cut up some bread, pour some grape juice, and quote the following Scripture.

He took some bread and gave thanks to God for it. Then he broke it in pieces and gave it to the disciples, saying, "This is my body, which is given for you. Do this to remember me." After supper he took another cup of wine and said, "This cup is the new covenant between God and his people—an agreement confirmed with my blood, which is poured out as a sacrifice for you" (Luke 22:19-20 NLT).

What can I say? It's a very precious time you are spending with the Lord.

What happens if I sin?

What happens if you sin after you've been forgiven? You know, there will be times—believe me—when you and I will mess up and sin against God. As Christians, we will eventually stumble. Only Jesus was perfect, but because we now have a new nature, it bothers us when sin.

But when people keep on sinning, it shows they belong to the Devil, who has been sinning since the beginning. But the Son of God came to destroy these works of the Devil. Those who have been born into God's family do not make a practice of sinning, because God's life is in them. So they can't keep on sinning, because they are children of God. (1 John 3:8-9 NLT)

I think that says it pretty clearly. You want to avoid all that sin and mess Jesus took you out of. It's simple—we *all* occasionally sin, but when we do, we ask forgiveness, stop doing the sin, and go on living victoriously. But know this—God still loves us even when we disobey Him. Do you stop loving your kids when they disobey you? Of course not. But our disobedience to God opens the door for the Devil to attack us. You may still make it to heaven, but you will live a defeated life here.

Salvation is not based on what we have done but on what Jesus did on the cross.

No, you don't need to get saved again. You don't get kicked out of the family of God because of sin. Someone who is truly born again will not want to continue in sin. Got it?

When you mess up, all you have to do is ask God to forgive you right on the spot. If you really mean it, He will. Jesus said, "But if we confess our sins to Him, he is faithful and just to forgive us our sins and to cleanse us from all wickedness" (1 John1:9 NLT). You don't have to go to someone else, like a priest, to have him go to God for you. No, you can and must go to God yourself, and He will instantly forgive you and cleanse you. You see, Jesus already paid the price for our sins. He tells us in other Scriptures to come to Him. Jesus said, "However, those the Father has given me will come to me, and I will *never reject them"* (John 6:37 NLT). *Never, never, never!*

There's still more great news. Look at what God says: "And He (God) has identified us as his own by placing the Holy Spirit in our hearts as the first installment that *guarantees* everything He has promised us" (2 Cor. 1:22 NLT). That cleansing you felt, that awesome peace in your heart when you asked Him to forgive you of your sins was His precious Holy Spirit (your Comforter, Counselor, and Best Friend) now living inside of you. You don't ever have to feel lonely again because He is *always* with you, even when you mess up. He said He would *never* leave you nor forsake you.

How does God do it? I don't know! I just know *He does*! Jesus said that with God all things are possible. When you received Jesus as your Lord and Savior, He gave you His Holy Spirit as proof that everything the Bible promises you is *yours*!

How do I handle criticism from friends and family about my newfound faith?

When you get saved and give your life to Jesus, frequently you still have to return to the place and things that caused you to sin in the first place. You may have to go back to your home to your family that doesn't know the Lord, back to friends who sinned with you, or back to the environment that caused you to be separated from God. The problems and troubles are still there! You are different, but they are the same. So how do you deal with that?

First of all, remember that *you* are a new person now. God now lives inside of you, guiding you, strengthening you, and teaching you. Family and friends may not understand your new life. They may laugh and ridicule you. That's because they don't know the Lord and are still in the darkness that God just delivered you from.

Well, all you can do is: (1) Tell them about your newfound freedom in Christ and how for the first time in your life, you have peace, love, and joy and are a different person. Tell them that now you can love them more than ever because God, who is love, lives inside of you. (2) Tell them that Jesus can do the same for them. Everyone is seeking to fill that emptiness in their life, but only God can do that. (3) Then, in your prayer time, pray for them that God would use you or send someone else to tell them about salvation. (4) Above all, love them—show them the love of Jesus.

After we got saved, we were so happy and excited that we went to visit my mom and sister in NYC and told them about Jesus. They also gave their hearts and lives to Jesus. Sometimes you have to pray for a while to get someone to accept Jesus as their Savior, but don't give up! God is faithful to answer our prayers! Also, remember this: you don't have to make drastic changes in your new life. Let God lead you. Believe me, He will tell you what to change in your life.

I also was a smoker when I came to the Lord, and I had desperately tried to quit smoking for years and had no success. I was young and with a small child and did not want those stupid cigarettes to kill me. After I got saved, I still smoked because I hadn't learned yet how to get rid of the nasty habit.

One day in church the pastor was up on the pulpit preaching, and he happened to say, "Do you know that there are no cigarette stores in heaven?" Nobody in the church knew I smoked. Nobody. I knew it must be God talking to me cause nobody knew! I went home that night and thought about what the pastor said. Just that one sentence made me think.

"Wow," I said. "Then where in heaven am I going to get my Winstons?" Before going to bed, I prayed, "Lord, if You take away my *craving* and *desire* for cigarettes, I promise you I will do the rest." End of prayer. I didn't say anything else and went to bed, but I meant every word I said. The next morning, when I went to reach for my cigarettes as usual after my morning coffee, guess what? I had absolutely *no* desire for that cigarette. None. Zippo. Nada. Like I promised the Lord, I threw them suckers away and never again picked up a cigarette. I'm telling you, God answers prayer!

Must I forgive everyone?

Yup! The Bible says that if we don't forgive, we will not be forgiven. That means I will not go to heaven because I knowingly hold something in my heart against someone. If you've searched your heart and honestly can't remember holding any grudges against anyone, then that's okay. But guess what? The Holy Spirit living inside of you *will* remind you of any ill feelings you may still have, and then you will have *no* choice but to forgive.

"But listen here," you may say, "you don't know what that so-and-so did to me. I will never forgive him/her. Why the pain is so great, it's like it happened yesterday." I know what you're saying. I hear ya. But God is very, very clear that we must forgive. Listen to what He says: "Make allowance for each other's faults, and forgive anyone who offends you. Remember, the Lord forgave you, so you must forgive others" (Colossians 3:13 NLT).

In Matthew 18, Jesus talks about a master who forgave his servant a huge debt (like a million dollars). This servant had a coworker who owed him around twenty bucks. Do you know what this servant did? He had the coworker thrown in jail for non-payment. When the master found out what this servant had done, he said to him that if he, the master, had shown compassion to him by forgiving his huge debt, he should have done the same to this fellow servant. The master was very angry and had this wicked servant delivered to the torturers.

Do you know what Jesus said then? Let me say it exactly as He said it: "So My heavenly Father also will do to you if each of you, *from his heart*, does not forgive his brother his trespasses" (Matthew 18:35 NKJV). Listen, nobody—and I mean nobody—is worth going to hell for. Life has enough challenges here on this earth. Then are we going miss heaven too? No, I don't think so.

Do you realize that when you don't forgive, you eat and sleep that person?

That person is probably not thinking about you, but you are being tormented by the thoughts of what he or she did to you. It's time to let go. I've personally had a *lot* of folks come against me. What hurt the most was it was mostly people I loved, close friends and even family! We have to say what Jesus said when He was nailed to the cross: "Father, forgive them, for they don't know what they are doing" (Luke 23:34 NLT). If He—who was perfect and sinless and never, never, never hurt *anyone*, but only loved and healed all those He who needed Him—forgave, how much more do we have to forgive. You and I are not perfect. We've hurt other people—maybe not always on purpose, but we have.

Unforgiveness is ugly. It's a burden, and it will keep you from being blessed. Still not convinced? A couple of years ago, some people I loved came against my husband and me big time, and I became very angry and bitter. Even though I knew everything I am telling you, I allowed myself to—and even enjoyed—intensely dislike them. Sorry,

I'm just being real with you. I never actually said I hated them, but in my heart, I was very, very angry.

Well, several weeks went by, and I was sitting in church on a Sunday morning. Then all of a sudden, with my eyes open, I saw a short video of me being angry and bitter with a neighbor a few days earlier. She was the head of my neighborhood association. My husband was outside cutting grass that day, and she came by and told him that the flowers in my yard were against association regulations and that because I didn't get the association's permission, I might have to remove them.

What? Who did she think she was? When he told me that, I went off and told him, "It's a good thing she hadn't said it to me or we would have been rolling on the grass!" He didn't get upset at her, but I was furious! I called her a fat slob, and then I yelled at *him* for not yelling at *her*!

Well, there I was sitting in church, listening to the pastor speak. He happened to be speaking about bitterness and unforgiveness, but I knew he wasn't talking about me! I was in denial. So I saw this video in my head and heard a voice say (I could hear the voice inside of me, not with my ears), "Yes, he is speaking about you because you are angry and bitter."

I said, "Yes, Lord. Forgive me. I will forgive them too and let go of those feelings." So, I went up to the altar and prayed and left all that mess there.

You see, that anger and bitterness inside of me caused me to be angry and bitter with *everyone*. That's what unforgiveness does. It's like poison. Man, I let go of that junk quick, but in reality, I was the one who was freed! I felt peace. Wow. It was great. My whole attitude changed. I was back to my normal self. Unforgiveness changes you and makes you ugly inside.

Sometimes forgiving someone involves going to that person and asking him or her to forgive you. Oh, yeah. That's when it gets hard. I've done that too. If the Lord tells you to do it, you've gotta do it. Sometimes people will use this opportunity to say nasty things to you since they see you are sorry. But listen, if they accept your apology, great. If they don't, who cares! You did what pleased God, and now you are free! If they didn't accept your apology, that's their problem. Your mind and heart are clear, and that's all that matters. Even if the person that hurt you has died or you cannot reach them, *let it go*. Give all of those hurt feelings to Jesus and let Him carry them for you.

Don't wait any longer. Forgive—from your heart—those who have come against you, for God has too many great things in store for you. Forgiveness means you no longer remember what they did to you. That's how God forgives us, and that's how we must forgive. Don't let anyone keep you from your blessings!

Filet Mignon

And now for what I call the filet mignon—Scriptures that will encourage and motivate you. It's like when you eat a good steak. Chew on these and meditate on them during the day, slowly enjoying their flavor! God's words are like bullets in your gun (mouth), so speak them out loud. Fire them at the Devil and whatever comes against you.

Psalm 91 (read daily)

Those who live in the shelter of the Most High will find rest in the shadow of the Almighty. This I declare about the LORD: He alone is my refuge, my place of safety; he is my God, and I trust him. For he will rescue you from every trap and protect you from deadly disease. He will cover you with his feathers. He will shelter you with his wings. His faithful promises are your armor and protection. Do not be afraid of the terrors of the night, nor the arrow that flies in the day. Do not dread the disease that stalks in darkness, nor the disaster that strikes at midday. Though a thousand fall at your side, though ten thousand are dying around you, these evils will not touch you. Just open your eyes, and see how the wicked are punished. If you make the LORD your refuge, if you make the Most High your shelter, no evil will conquer you; no plague will come near your home. For he will order his angels to protect you wherever you go. They will hold you up with their hands so you won't even hurt your foot on a stone. You will trample upon lions and cobras; you will crush fierce lions and serpents under your feet! The LORD says, "I will rescue those who love me. I will protect those who trust in my name. When they call on me, I will answer; I will be with them in trouble. I will rescue and honor them. I will reward them with a long life and give them my salvation (Psalm 91 NLT).

When you feel discouraged, this is one of my top ten favorites. Jesus said:

Behold I give *you* the authority to trample on serpents and scorpions and to overcome all of the power of the enemy and *nothing* shall by *any means* hurt you. (Luke 10:19 NKJV)

Those promises are yours. Speak them. Claim them. Stand on them.

Prayer of Salvation

Maybe you are reading this and have never given your life to Jesus. You've tried everything the world has to offer, yet inside nothing satisfies—you are still empty. That's how I felt. Well, my friend, it's not too late. Let me tell you, nothing can fill that vacant spot in your heart and soul but Jesus. No drugs, no alcohol, no sex, no person, no money—nothing can satisfy that void. Jesus loves you and wants to change your life. He died to set you free! Right now where you are, pray these words:

> Father, in the name of Jesus, I ask You to forgive me of all of my sins. I believe You sent Jesus to die for me and You raised Him from the dead. Jesus, come into my heart as my Lord and Savior, and change my life. I will live for You from this day forward. Amen.

If you really meant that, Jesus has come into your heart and soul, and you are now a child of God. Remember what I said. Find a church, get a Bible, talk to Him. He will hear you! God bless you!

Now you know where to go from here. I pray that this book has been of some help to you. I've shared my experiences and hopefully saved you from making some of the stupid mistakes I've made. So now you know.

God bless you, my brother/sister. I'll meet you in heaven one day, but meanwhile, live the abundant and victorious life that Jesus said He came to bring you and me. Enjoy Him—enjoy, enjoy, enjoy!

Go for it!